PIONEER PHOTO AL...

TOP LOADING SCRAPBOOKS

NEW! COVER DESIGNS

Sewn Scroll • Textured Mulberry • Printed Designer • Plaid Fabric • Embossed Mulberry • Bonded Leather • Gingham Fabric • Sewn Denim • Safari Faux Fur • Sewn Padded • Tapestry Fabric • 3-D Appliqué • 3-D Wedding • White Fabric • Frame Wedding • Striped Fabric • Diamond Fabric • Leather Bond Frame

Family Treasures®
Deluxe E-Z Load® Memory Scrapbooks

TRUE 12"x12" 8½"x11" 8"x8" 6"x6" 5"x7" 12"x15"

- **FABRIC HEAVY PADDED COVERS**
- **TOP LOADING POST-BOUND**
- **ROUNDED CORNERS**
- **EXPANDABLE ROUND SPINE**
- **REINFORCED HOLE PROTECTORS**

New Sizes! 8"x8" & 6"x6"

ARCHIVAL
ACID, PVC & LIGNIN FREE

White or black refills fit all Pioneer® post-bound E-Z Load® Memory Books, most staple-strap style or 3-ring memory books

REINFORCED POST BINDING TAKES UNLIMITED REFILLS • PAGES LAY FLAT
20 TOP LOADING PAGES INCLUDED
10 PLASTIC SHEET PROTECTORS WITH 10 WHITE PAPER INSERTS

Patent No. 6027140
Others Pending

Adhesives

ACID FREE

| Photo Sticker Captions | 3-D Gold, Silver or Black Letters | Rainbow Photo Corners | Metallic Photo Corners | Clear Photo Corners | Black Photo Corners | 1/4 Size Mini-Mounts | Photo Mounts 250 or 500 | Double Sided Tape | Permanent or Removable Roller Tape | Photo Glue Stick in 2 Sizes | Photo Glue Stick Pen | Photo Square Glue Stick |

Pioneer Photo Albums, Inc.

9801 Deering Ave • Chatsworth, CA 91311 • 800-366-3686 • 818-882-2161 • Fax 8188826239 • pioneer@pioneerphotoalbums.com

PIONEER Photo Albums

on the cover

HEY, THANKS!

Dana Smith of Eden Prairie, Minnesota

Cardstock: Bazzill Basics
Pattern Paper: Chatterbox
Ribbon: Unknown
Woven Label: Making Memories
Finished size: 5 1/2" x 4 1/4"

Special Thanks to Bassett Furniture of Orem, Utah

Publisher Chad Harvie

Editor in Chief Pam Baird

Assistant Editor Tammy Morrill

Contributing Editor/Designer Jeri Huish

Editorial Staff
Kara Henry and Jeannette Jones

Art Director Amy Noorda

Designer Linda Nelson

Photography Amanda Peterson

Contributers
Sophia Corbridge and Tina Gonzales

Retail Sales Manager
Amanda Peck
888-225-9199 x15
amandap@scrapbooktrendsmag.com

Retail Sales
Staci Vest
888-225-9199 x18
staciv@scrapbooktrendsmag.com

Subscriptions/Customer Service Alisha Gordon

Shipping/Receiving
Justin Woods and Tina Gonzales

Internet Customer Service
support@scrapbooktrendsmag.com

Advertising
Jan Rudd
888-225-9199 x12
janr@scrapbooktrendsmag.com

Amber Hall
888-225-9199 x14
amberh@scrapbooktrendsmag.com

Scrapbook Trends Magazine is published 12 times
a year by Northridge Media, LLC.
P.O. Box 1570 Orem, Utah 84059-1570
phone **888-225-9199** fax **801-225-6510**
e-mail: support@scrapbooktrendsmag.com
www.scrapbooktrendsmag.com

Subscriptions 1-888-225-9199
1 year U.S. subscription price: $24.97
2 year U.S. subscription price $44.97
3 year U.S. subscription price $62.97
1 year Canada/Mexico $40.97 (U.S. funds only)
Please call for other international rates.

Please send address changes to:
Northridge Media
P.O. Box 1570
Orem, Utah 84059-1570
or e-mail: support@scrapbooktrendsmag.com

Please send reader submissions to:
submissions@scrapbooktrendsmag.com,
submit@scrapbooktrendsmag.com, or
readers@scrapbooktrendsmag.com

Visit us online at:
scrapbooktrendsmag.com

contents

The Love Inside 96
Shortcuts to Fabulous Cards
by Sophia Corbridge

Babies 8
Birthday 22
Christmas 34
Congratulations 44
For my Friend 50
Get Well 60
Holidays 68
Invitations 76
Cards for Kids 82
Love & Romance 88
Quick & Easy 102
Sympathy 108
Thank You 112

From the Editor 7
Retail Store Directory 125
Advertising Directory 128

Scrapbook Trends Magazine (ISSN: 1532-4338) is published monthly for $24.97 per year by Northridge Media, LLC., 1442 East 820 North, Orem UT 84097. Periodicals Postage Paid at Orem UT and at additional mailing offices. POSTMASTER: Send Address changes to Scrapbook Trends Magazine, P.O. Box 1570, Orem UT 84059-1570

"You give but little when you give of your possessions. It is when you give of yourself that you truly give."

-Gibran

My family is lucky enough to live in a university town, and along with the cultural events it attracts to the community, the university also brings many visitors as they drop off or pick up students. This year my husband's cousin, Mary Lou, brought her 19 year old daughter for her first year at school. We enjoyed two evenings of catching up on the past several years and renewing family ties.

The next week I opened my mail box to find an envelope from Mary Lou. It was so exciting to see that it was card she had made especially for me! Although a thank you was not necessary for time together I'm sure we enjoyed even more than she did, it touched my heart and strengthened our connection.

When you spend the time and put in the effort to make a hand made card for someone, you truly are giving them a piece of yourself and expressing your well wishes. From thank yous to new babies to holidays, and everything in between, a home made card is sure to send the message that you truly do care!

We are excited to bring you Cards & Tags 2005! Our contributors and readers have submitted fabulous cards to bring you lots of ideas for every occasion. Enjoy leafing through the pages, mark your favorites, and get ready to make some terrific cards!

Pam

BABY

Susan Weinroth
of Philadelphia, Pennsylvania

Cardstock: Bazzill Basics
Safety pin: Making Memories
Ribbon: Offray
Cutouts: Foofala
Stickers: Pebbles, Inc.
Finished size: 5" x 5"

Try using a variety of techniques when creating a card to add visual interest. Stitching, tearing, and curling the edges have combined to make this a charming card for baby.

EMBRACE
Tina Gonzales

Cardstock: Bazzill Basics
Pattern paper: American Crafts
Charm: Making Memories
Wood frame: Li'l Davis Designs
Sticker: Creative Imaginations
Ribbon: May Arts
Finished size: 5" x 5"

SUGAR AND SPICE
Summer Ford
of San Antonio, Texas

Cardstock: The Paper Company
Pattern paper: Design Originals
Bottle caps: Li'l Davis Designs
Ribbon: May Arts
Punch: Fiskars
Ink: Ranger
Finished size: 5" x 4 1/4"

A PIECE OF HEAVEN

Robin Hohenstern
of Brooklyn Park,
Minnesota

Cardstock: Wausau
Pattern paper, stickers
and twill words:
Carolee's Creations
Ribbon: Offray
Font: McBoo by Hallmark
Finished size: 4" x 5 1/4"

Robin printed
the picture onto
cardstock for a
textured look.

BABY

Stefanie Gillins
of Minersville, Utah

Cardstock: Bazzill Basics
Stickers: Pebbles, Inc.
Ribbon: Offray
Finished size: 6" x 5"

BABY GIRL

Amy O'Neil of Chandler, Arizona

Pattern paper and tags: Rusty Pickle
Eyelets: Creative Imaginations
Pin: Making Memories
Chipboard, ribbon and paint: Unknown
Rub ons: Chatterbox
Stickers: EK Success
Ink: Ranger
Clear medium: Diamond Glaze
Finished size: 4 1/4" x 2 1/2"

Amy painted a chipboard frame with pink paint, let it dry, sanded the edges and sealed it with clear glaze.

CONGRATS

by Terri Davenport
of Toledo, Ohio

Cardstock:
Pebbles in my Pocket
Transparency: Office supply
Metal frame: Scrapworks
Safety pins and ribbon:
Making Memories
Stamps: Hero Arts
Ink: Stampin' Up!
and Hero Arts
Finished size: 3 1/4" x 4"

BABY PHOTO BOOK

Vicki Harvey
of Champlin, Minnesota

Cardstock: Pebbles, Inc.
Pattern paper: Melissa Frances
and Mustard Moon
Charms: Artsy Tartsy
Brad and paint: Making Memories
Jump ring: Darice
Perforated letters: Mustard Moon
Twill: Creative Imaginations
Rub ons: Chatterbox
Stickers: Melissa Frances
Ink: Ranger
Braided trim and flower: Craft supply
Finished size: 5 1/2" x 6"

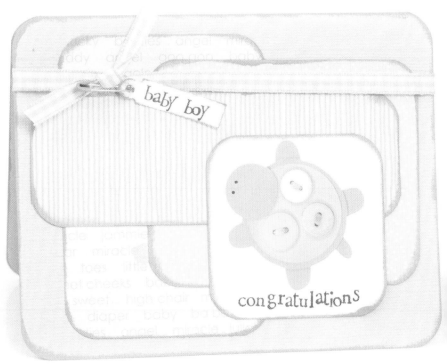

CONGRATULATIONS BABY BOY

Tania Willis of Canton, Ohio

Keep a variety of needles on hand so that you'll have the right needle for the task. Use needles to stitch threads onto your cards, to sew buttons or to attach beads.

Cardstock: **Bazzill Basics**
Pattern paper and stickers:
Doodlebug Design
Safety pin, tags and paint:
Making Memories
Ribbon: **Offray**
Punch: **EK Success**
Stamps: **Hero Arts**
Ink: **Ranger**
Finished size: 4 1/4" x 5 1/2"

IT'S A BOY

Alisha Gordon

Cardstock: **Bazzill Basics**
Pattern paper: **My Mind's Eye**
Rub ons and fiber:
Making Memories
Finished size: 5" x 4 1/2"

BABY
Kelli Dickinson of Des Moines, Iowa

Cardstock: Bazzill Basics
Pattern paper: me & my BIG ideas
Brads: Lasting Impressions
Tokens: Doodlebug Design
Ribbon: houseofpaper.com
Stickers: Alphabilities
Ink: Versacolor
Finished size: 7" x 5"

PRECIOUS
Cindy Harris of Modesto, California

Cardstock, pattern paper
and stickers: Pebbles, Inc.
Ribbon: Queen & Co.
Finished size: 3 1/2" x 5"

Transparent buttons or tokens enhance the look of the pattern paper.

PRECIOUS BOY

Stacey Kingman
of Ellsworth, Illinois

Cardstock: Bazzill Basics
Pattern paper: Chatterbox
Ribbon: May Arts and Offray
Punches: Fiskars
Stickers: Paper Bliss
Ink: Ranger
Label maker: Dymo
Finished size: 4 1/4" x 5 1/2"

Pull out forgotten border templates or decorative scissors for a finished border on your cards.

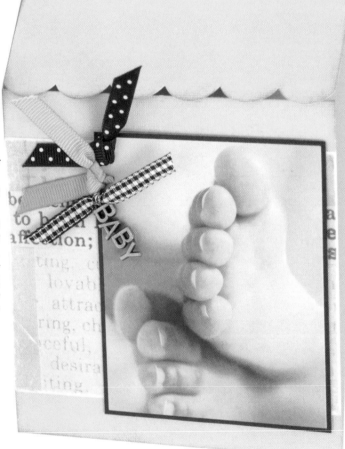

BABY

Cindy Smith of Knoxville, Maryland

Cardstock: Bazzill Basics
and Die Cuts with a View
Pattern paper: Pebbles, Inc.
Charms: Karen Foster
Ribbon: Offray and Stampin' Up!
Ink: Versacolor
Finished size: 5 1/2" x 4 1/4"

CONGRATULATIONS!

Karen Thaemert
of Saint Charles, Missouri

Cardstock and ink: Stampin' Up!
Pattern paper and rub ons:
me & my BIG ideas
Vellum: Keller Creations
Eyelets: The Eyelet Outlet
Mesh: Magic Mesh
Ribbon: Unknown
Tags: Making Memories
Stickers: Creative Imaginations
Finished size: 4 1/4" x 5 1/2"

Remember to check your sewing supplies when making cards. You might find just the right leftover trim to add the perfect touch. And keep your sewing machine handy; sewing is as attractive on cards as it is on layouts!

OH BABY!

Monica Anderson
of Glendale, Arizona

Cardstock: Bazzill Basics
Pattern paper:
Creative Imaginations
Rub ons: KI Memories
Stickers: Doodlebug Design
and Pebbles, Inc.
Slide holders: scrapsahoy.com
Ric rac: Craft supply
Finished size: 4 1/2" x 5 1/2"

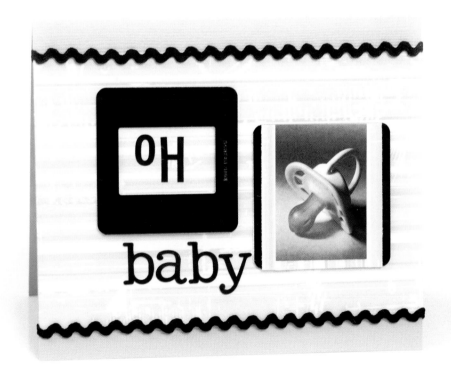

BABY BOY
Tina Gonzales

Cardstock: Bazzill Basics
Ribbon: May Arts
Hand charm: Dress It Up
Clear sticker: It Takes Two
Finished size: 4" x 4 1/4" closed
8" x 4 1/4" open

even before the stars
lit up the sky, your
little boy
had a special place
in the heart of God.

we welcome your new
baby with joy!

BABY BOY POCKET
Tina Gonzales

Pocket: Kopp Design
Rub ons: Meta Fora
Icicle word: KI Memories
Font: Quirky, downloaded from
twopeasinabucket.com
Finished size: 5 1/4" x 3 1/2"

Kolby Bryan Gonzales

Sept. 26th, 2004

Proud parents:
Bryan and Tamra
7 lbs 8oz

babies

BABY
Alisha Gordon

Cardstock: Bazzill Basics
Tacks: Chatterbox
Die cuts: My Mind's Eye
Flower: Making Memories
Finished size: 5" x 6"

Think outside the box! The center of the flower doesn't always have to be a circle.

BABY
Sophia Corbridge

Pattern paper: O'Scrap!
Rub on: Making Memories
Lettering: SEI
Page pebbles: EK Success
Finished size: 6" x 6"

NEW BABY

Robin Hohenstern
of Brooklyn Park, Minnesota

Cardstock: **Wausau**
Pattern paper and stickers:
Carolee's Creations
Charms: **Memory Shoppe**
Ribbon: **Offray**
Finished size: 4 1/4" x 5 1/4"

BABY

Alisha Gordon

Cardstock: **Bazzill Basics**
Pattern paper: **Frances Meyer**
Rub ons and metal plaque:
Making Memories
Ribbon: **Offray**
Flowers: **Jolee's Boutique**
Finished size: 5" x 4 3/4"

BABY, BABY, BABY

Robin Hohenstern
of Brooklyn Park, Minnesota

Cardstock: Wausau
Pattern paper, ribbon
and shaker: Carolee's Creations
Safety pin: Making Memories
Finished size: 4 1/4" x 5"

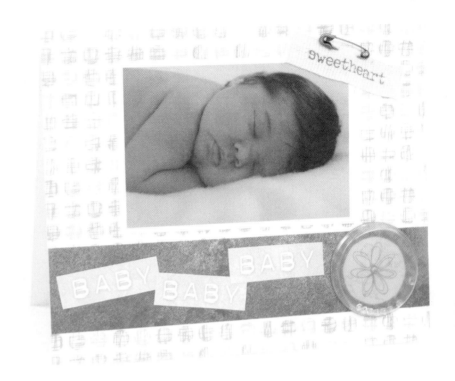

A BOY IS A JOY

Sophia Corbridge

Pattern paper: Alphaworks and O'Scrap!
Tag: All My Memories
Twill tape: Creative Images
Brads: Bazzill Basics
Stickers: Alphaworks
Ink: Close To My Heart
Finished size: 6" x 6"

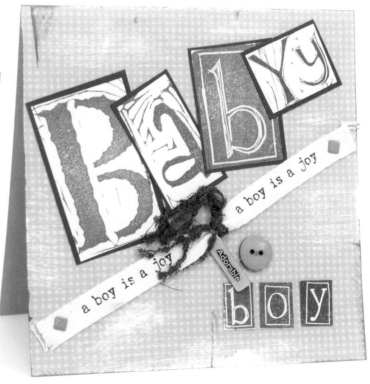

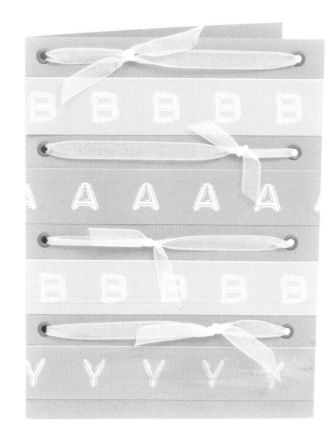

BABY

Sophia Corbridge

Cardstock: **Bazzill Basics**
Eyelets: **Making Memories**
Stickers: **Alphaworks**
Ribbon: **Offray**
Finished size: 5 1/2" x 4 1/4"

Inside

BABY

Terry Koehler of Olathe, Kansas

Pattern paper and label: **Rebecca Sower**
Charm: **American Traditional Designs**
Safety pins, ribbon and brad: **Craft supply**
Stamps: **Printworks**
Finished size: 5 1/2" x 4 1/4"

SMALLL WONDER
Terry Koehler of Olathe, Kansas

Pattern paper and label:
Rebecca Sower for EK Success
Charm: American Traditional Designs
Brad and ribbon: Unknown
Stamps: Printworks
Finished size: 5 1/2" x 4 1/4"

Inside

Personalize the card by putting the new baby's name on it!

WELCOME TO THE WORLD
Dustin Nakamura
of Rocklin, California

Cardstock: Bazzill Basics,
Making Memories
and Die Cuts with a View
Pattern paper: KI Memories
Vellum: Stampin' Up!
Brads and photo turn:
Making Memories
Ribbon: May Arts
Ink: ColorBox
Fonts: David Walker Curls and Swirls,
downloaded from
twopeasinabucket.com
Finished size: 5" x 6 3/4"

HAPPY BIRTHDAY TAG

Gina Regala of San Jose, California

Cardstock: Bazzill Basics
Pattern paper: American Crafts
Ribbon: May Arts
Die cuts: Second Avenue
Punch: Creative Memories
Templates: Adobe Illustrator
Font: Walrod, downloaded from dafont.com
Finished size: 6 1/2" x 3 1/2"

Gina printed the letter S onto green cardstock in reverse, then cut it out with an exacto knife.

HAPPY BIRTHDAY TO YOU
Wendy Malichio of Bethel, Connecticut

Pattern paper: Die Cuts with a View
Brads and bookplate: Joann's Scrap Essentials
Staples: Office supply
Punch: EK Success
Ribbon: Craft supply
Paint: Americana
Fonts: Arial and Cornerstone
Finished size: 5 1/2" x 8"

Use a bookplate to highlight the message you want to convey. Try placing it over the text on pattern paper with repeated text.

HAPPY BIRTHDAY, BELLE
Alisha Gordon

Card, tag, silver brad and ribbon:
Making Memories
Pattern paper: SEI
Pink brad: Provo Craft
Rub on: Scrap-Rub
Font: Dot by PC Craft
Finished size: 4 1/4" x 5 1/4"

HAPPY BIRTHDAY
Sophia Corbridge

Cardstock: O'Scrap!
Pattern paper and brads:
Carolee's Creations
Rub on: Making Memories
Boshers: Bazzill Basics
Stamps and ink: Close To My Heart
Finished size: 6" x 6"

HAPPY BIRTHDAY
Stefanie Gillins of Minersville, Utah

Cardstock: Bazzill Basics
Pattern paper: Chatterbox
Stamp: Hero Arts
Button: Creative Imaginations
Finished size: 5 1/4" x 4"

HAPPY BIRTHDAY 2U

Stacey Kingman
of Ellsworth, Illinois

Cardstock: **Bazzill Basics**
Pattern paper, acrylic accents
and die cuts: **KI Memories**
Staples: **Office supply**
Ribbon: **Offray and May Arts**
Stickers: **Doodlebug Design**
Ink: **Ranger**
Label maker: **Dymo**
Finished size: 4" x 5 1/2"

By intentionally placing the letters in a whimsical fashion, there's no need to worry about keeping them perfectly aligned.

BUTTERFLY CARD AND TAG SET

Karen Bukovan
of Odessa, Florida

Cardstock: **Bazzill Basics**
Stickers: **Kathy Davis**
Stamps: **Hero Arts**
and **Stampin' Up!**
Ribbon: **Craft supply**
Finished size: 5 1/2" x 4 1/4"

Create a gift tag to match your card!

HAPPY BIRTHDAY
Alisha Gordon

Cardstock: **Bazzill Basics**
Pattern paper: **American Crafts**
Brads, staples and ribbon:
Making Memories
Rub ons: **Scrap-Ease**
Finished size: 5 1/4" x 5 1/4"

Using staples is a quick and easy way to attach ribbons and fibers. Not only is it a great look, but will also save you time.

HAPPY BIRTHDAY GRAM
Alissa Fast
of Ferndale, Washington

Cardstock: **French Paper Co.**
Pattern paper: **SEI**
Brads: **American Tag Co.**
Stickers: **K & Company**
Woven label: **Making Memories**
Flowers: **Craft supply**
Ink: **ColorBox**
Finished size: 5" x 4 1/4"

HAPPY BIRTHDAY ANGELA

Gayle Hodgins
of Philadelphia, Pennsylvania

Cardstock: Bazzill Basics
Pattern paper: K & Company
Brad and safety pin: The Happy Hammer
Clip: Junkitz
Acrylic flower: KI Memories
Ribbon: Lifetime Moments
Die cuts: My Mind's Eye
Stickers: K & Company
and me & my BIG ideas
Ink: Ranger
Finished size: 6" x 6"

HAPPY BIRTHDAY

Alisha Gordon

Cardstock: Bazzill Basics
Pattern paper: American Craft
Brads and ribbon: Making Memories
Rub ons: Scrap-Ease
Finished size: 5" x 4"

HAPPY BIRTHDAY ACCORDION CARD

Alissa Fast of Ferndale, Washington

Cardstock: Pebbles in my Pocket
Pattern paper: Rusty Pickle
and Mustard Moon
Brads: Making Memories
Book plate: Li'l Davis Designs
Ribbon: Offray
Slide mount: Design Originals
Dominoes: 7 Gypsies
Stickers: Creative Imaginations,
Doodlebug Design, Making Memories,
Pebbles, Inc. and Li'l Davis Designs
Ink: Nick Bantock
Finished size: 4" x 6"

HAPPY BIRTHDAY
Tina Gonzales

Cardstock: **Bazzill Basics**
Pattern paper: **Chatterbox**
Charm: **Making Memories**
Punch: **Family Treasures**
Stamp and ink: **Close To My Heart**
Finished size: 4 1/4" x 6 1/4"

HAPPY BIRTHDAY 2 U
Mary Jo Johnston
of Lafayette, Indiana

Cardstock: **The Paper Company**
Pattern paper: **7 Gypsies, Collage Papers and The Paper Loft**
Brads: **Creative Impressions**
Ribbon: **May Arts**
Rub ons: **Wordsworth**
Stickers: **K & Company**
Ink: **Ranger**
Finished size: 5 1/2" x 4"

CELEBRATE
Tracy Michelitch
of Ashburn, Virginia

Pattern paper and tag:
KI Memories
Brads: Bazzill Basics
Photo turns: 7 Gypsies
Rub ons: Making Memories
Finished size: 5" x 7"

HAPPY BIRTHDAY
Ralonda Heston
of Murfreesboro, Tennesse

Pattern paper and stickers: Basic Grey
Ribbon: Fibers By the Yard
Font: Caslon 540, downloaded from the internet

HAPPY BIRTHDAY
Terry Koehler of Olathe, Kansas

Pattern paper: SEI
Corrugated paper, fabric, brads
and party hat: Unknown
Stamps: Printworks
Finished size: 5 1/2" x 4 1/4"

HAPPY BIRTHDAY
Becky Novacek of Fremont, Nebraska

Card base, tag, file folder tab and ticket: Foofala
Pattern paper: me & my BIG ideas and Anna Griffin
Photo corners: Canson
Brads: Making Memories
Photo turn: 7 Gypsies
Ribbon: May Arts
Rub ons: Autumn Leaves
Stamps: Ma Vinci's Reliquary, Hero Arts and PSX
Ink: ColorBox
Pen: Zig
Finished size: 5" x 6"

Inside

Premade file folders are a great beginning for a card!

SPECIAL DAY
Stacey Kingman
of Ellsworth, Illinois

Cardstock: Bazzill Basics
Pattern paper, die cuts, acrylic accents and stickers: KI Memories
Brads: Making Memories
Staples: Office supply
Ribbon: May Arts, me & my BIG ideas and Leeza Gibbons
Ink: Ranger
Label maker: Dymo
Finished size: 6" x 6"

MY FABULOUS FRIEND
Alissa Fast of Ferndale, Washington

Cardstock: French Paper Co. and Bazzill Basics
Pattern paper: SEI
Ribbon: May Arts
Ink: Nick Bantock
Font: Autumn Leaves Outdoors, downloaded from
twopeasinabucket.com and Hannibal Lector,
downloaded from the internet
Finished size: 5 1/2" x 4 1/4"

HAPPY BIRTHDAY
TO YOU
Sophia Corbridge

Cardstock and boshers: Bazzill Basics
Pattern paper: Carolee's Creations
Brads: All My Memories
and Carolee's Creations
Tags: Making Memories
Stamps: Hero Arts
Ink: Close To My Heart
Finished size: 4 1/4" X 5 1/2"

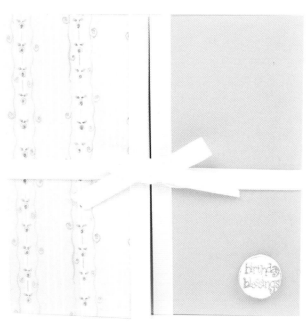

BIRTHDAY BLESSINGS
Sophia Corbridge

Cardstock: Bazzill Basics
Pattern paper: Creative Images
Tile: EK Success
Stamps and ink: Close To My Heart
Ribbon: Offray
Finished size: 6" x 6"

EAT CAKE
Karen Bukovan
of Odessa, Florida

Cardstock: Bazzill Basics
Stickers: Pebbles, Inc.
and me & my BIG ideas
Ribbon: Craft supply
Finished size: 5 1/2" x 4 1/4"

HAPPY BIRTHDAY
Tina Gonzales

Pattern paper: American Crafts
Charm: Making Memories
Punch: Family Treasures
Eyelets: Doodlebug Design
Finished size: 4" x 4"

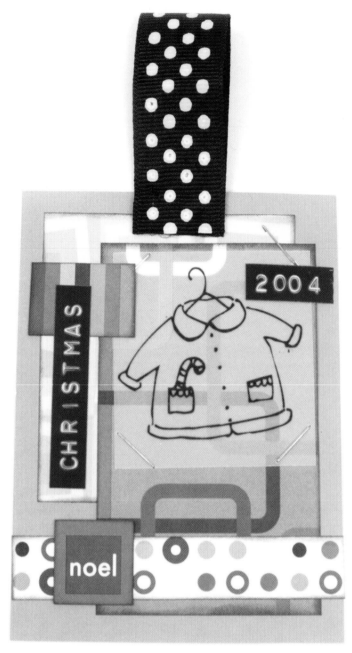

CHRISTMAS 2004

Dustin Nakamura of Rocklin, California

Cardstock, pattern paper and cutouts: KI Memories
Vellum: Stampin' Up!
Staples: Office supply
Ribbon: Offray
Label maker: Dymo
Finished size: 4 1/2" x 3 1/4"

BELIEVE
Amy O'Neil of Chandler, Arizona

Cardstock: Bazzill Basics
Pattern paper: Melissa Frances
Brads: Making Memories
Bookplate: houseofpaper.com
Rub ons: Making Memories
and Melissa Frances
Ink: Ranger and Nick Bantock
Finished size: 5" x 5"

Text paper is a page from a Nancy Drew book. Make a color copy or tear a page from an old book to make a quick and interesting background.

HO HO HO
Sophia Corbridge

Cardstock: Bazzill Basics
Pattern paper: Carolee's Creations
Stamps and ink: Close To My Heart
Buttons: SEI
Floss: DMC
Finished size: 4 1/4" x 5 1/2"

JINGLE

Susan Weinroth
of Philadelphia, Pennsylvania

Cardstock and brads: Bazzill Basics
Pattern paper: KI Memories
Bell: Craft supply
Ribbon: May Arts
Rub ons: Making Memories
Ink: Ranger
Finished size: 4 3/4" x 6"

CHRISTMAS TAG

Dustin Nakamura of Rocklin, California

Cardstock: Bazzill Basics
Pattern paper: KI Memories
Photo turn and stickers: Making Memories
Ribbon: May Arts
Ink: ColorBox
Vintage image: dowloaded from the internet
Finished size: 4 3/4" x 3 1/4"

FROM OUR FAMILY
TO YOURS

Tina Gonzales

Cardstock: Bazzill Basics
Pattern paper: Pebbles, Inc.
Sleigh: Paper Bliss
Stickers: Pebbles, Inc.
Finished size: 6" x 6"

HO, HO, HO
Sophia Corbridge

Cardstock: Bazzill Basics
Pattern paper: Paper Pizzazz
Brads: Carolee's Creations
Stamps and ink: PSX
Finished size: 6" x 6

Using corrugated paper creates a unique card base. Make sure to score the paper before folding.

MERRY CHRISTMAS
Vanessa Spady of Virginia Beach, Virginia

Card base: DMD
Cardstock: Unknown
Brads: Making Memories
Ribbon: Craft supply
Die cuts: EK Success
Stamps: Stampin' Up!
Pens: Krylon and Marvy Uchida
Watercolor pencils: Staedtler
Finished size: 5 1/2" x 4 1/4"

Inside

CHRISTMAS TAGBOOK

Sue Fields
of South Whitley, Indiana

Cardstock, pattern paper, charms
and die cuts: KI Memories
Brads: Creative Imaginations
Washer: Bazzill Basics
Ribbon: luvzscrapbook.com
Stickers: Bo Bunny Press
Finished size: (not including tabs)
  Page 1: 5 1/2"x 3 1/4"
  Page 2: 5"x 2"
  Page 3: 4"x 4"
  Page 4: 6 1/4"x 4 1/4"
  Page 5: 5 1/2"x 5"

MERRY CHRISTMAS

Miki Benedict
of Modesto, California

Cardstock: Bazzill Basics
Pattern paper and stickers:
KI Memories
Ric rac: Wrights
Finished size: 5" x 7"

MERRY CHRISTMAS

Terry Koehler of Olathe, Kansas

Pattern paper: Melissa Frances
Tissue paper, bag and clothes pin:
Craft supply
Stamps: Printworks
Finished size: 5 1/2" x 4 1/4"

To wish you
the gift of faith,
the blessing of hope and
the peace of His love
at christmas and always

inside

39

ENARSON CHRISTMAS CARD
Diane Enarson of Corona, California

Cardstock: Pebbles Inc.
Pattern paper: Provo Craft and Karen Foster
Safety pin, tree charm and tag: Making Memories
Ribbon: Offray
Ink: Ranger
Finished size: 4" x 5 1/2"

Machine stitching is a quick and easy way to add texture to a card.

HOLLY JOLLY
Tina Gonzales

Cardstock: Bazzill Basics
Pattern paper and sticker: Pebbles, Inc.
Charm, tag and metal word:
Making Memories
Finished size: 6" x 6"

HAPPY HOLIDAYS
Tina Gonzales

Cardstock: Bazzill Basics
Pattern paper: KI Memories
Stamp and ink: Hero Arts
Charm: Making Memories
Finished size: 4" x 4"

HAPPY HOLIDAYS TAG
Dustin Nakamura
of Rocklin, California

Cardstock: Die Cuts With a View
Pattern paper and cutouts: KI Memories
Vellum: Stampin' Up!
Staples: Office supply
Ribbon: May Arts
Ink: ColorBox
Label maker: Dymo
Finished size: 5" x 3 1/4"

HAPPY HOLIDAYS
Cindy Smith of Knoxville, Maryland

Cardstock: Stampin' Up!
Eyelets: Joann's Scrapbook Essentials
Stickers: Die Cuts With a View
Finished size: 5 1/2" x 4 1/4"

BUNDLE UP TIGHT

Cindy Smith
of Knoxville, Maryland

Cardstock: Bazzill Basics and Stampin' Up!
Pattern paper: Rusty Pickle
Stickers: All My Memories
Jute: Stampin' Up!
Finished size: 4 1/4" x 5 1/2"

WINTER

Kelly Sullivan
of Rochester, New York

Cardstock and pattern paper:
Die Cuts With a View
Charm and rub ons:
Making Memories
Ribbon: Offray
Paint: Folk Art
Finished size: 5" x 6"

SILVER TREES

Terry Koehler of Olathe, Kansas

Cardstock: **Bazzill Basics**
Pattern paper: **Creative Imaginations**
Ribbon and embossing powder: **Unknown**
Stamps: **Printworks and The Blue Hand**
Finished size: **7" x 5"**

To wish you
the gift of faith,
the blessing of hope and
the peace of His love
at christmas and always

inside

2004

Tina Gonzales

Cardstock: **Bazzill Basics**
Pattern paper: **American Traditional Designs**
Rub ons: **Making Memories**
Ribbon: **May Arts**
Finished size: **5" x 5"**

CONGRATS

Dana Smith of Eden Prairie, Minnesota

Cardstock: Bazzill Basics
Pattern paper, tacks and stencils: Chatterbox
Ribbon: Craft supply
Stickers: Memories
Stamps: Hero Arts
Finished size: 5 1/2" x 4 1/4"

CELEBRATE

Terry Koehler of Olathe, Kansas

Cardstock: Bazzill Basics
Pattern paper: Dictionary paper
Buttons: Craft supply
Stickers: Marcella by Kay
Stamps: Printworks
Finished size: 4 1/4" x 5 1/2"

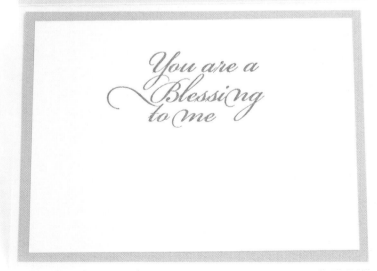

You are a Blessing to me

inside

CONGRATULATIONS!

Melanie Douthit of West Monroe, Louisiana

Cardstock: Bazzill Basics
Pattern paper: Chatterbox
Eyelets: Eyelets of the Month
Ribbon: Stampin' Up!
Punch: Fiskars
Stamp: Scrapgoods
Ink: Versamark
Embossing powder: Ranger
Finished size: 4 1/4" x 5 /2"

Repeating the border edge on the vellum, as well as the card edge, gives this card a very delicate, feminine touch.

CAPTURE THE MOMENT

Sophia Corbridge

Pattern paper: O'Scrap! and SEI
Label: All My Memories
Buttons: Dress It Up
Ink: Ranger
Ribbon: SEI
Finished Size: 6" X 6"

CELEBRATE
Sophia Corbridge

Cardstock: Bazzill Basics
Pattern paper: Carolee's Creations
Tag and clip: Making Memories
Stamps: Hero Arts and EK Success
Ink: Close To My Heart
Button: Jesse James
Chalk: Craf-T
Ribbon: SEI
Finished size: 5 1/2" x 4"

ENJOY
Sophia Corbridge

Pattern paper and ribbon: SEI
Label: All My Memories
Eyelet: Making Memories
Ink: Ranger
Finished size: 3 1/2" x 1 3/4"

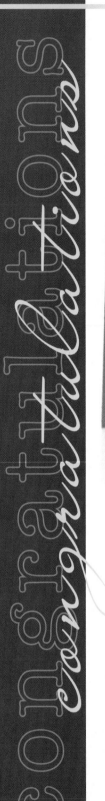

CLASS OF '05
Kristi Mangan
of West Palm Beach, Florida

Cardstock: Bazzill Basics
Pattern paper and stickers: KI Memories
Ric rac: Craft supply
Finished size: 5 1/2" x 6"

WAY TO GO
Sophia Corbridge

Pattern paper, vellum, ribbon
and stickers: SEI
Ink: Making Memories
Ribbon: Offray
Finished size: 4 1/4" x 5 1/2"

WAY TO GO!
Sophia Corbridge

Cardstock: Bazzill Basics
Pattern paper and ribbon: SEI
Clip: Making Memories
Pen: Zig
Finished size: 4 1/4" x 5 1/2"

Before inserting the tags into this pocket card, apply adhesive to the tags so that each tag, bearing the message, will stay in place.

HOW EXCITING FOR YOU!
Sophia Corbridge

Cardstock: Bazzill Basics
Pattern paper and sticker: Magenta
Clip: Carolee's Creations
Stamps and ink: Close To My Heart
Ribbon: Offray
Finished size: 6" x 6"

FRIENDSHIP

Teresa Brada of Elyria, Ohio

Cardstock: Bazzill Basics
Pattern paper: Anna Griffin
Vellum: Unknown
Bookplate: K & Company
Label: me & my BIG ideas
Ribbon: Making Memories and craft supply
Lace: Rebecca Sower
Punch: EK Success
Stamps: Stampin' Up!
Ink: ColorBox
Finished size: 5 1/2" x 4 1/4"

for my friend for my friend for my friend

FLOWERS

Amy Smith
of Los Angeles, California

Cardstock: Bazzill Basics
and Neenah
Ribbon: Offray
Tags: Making Memories
Stickers: Stickopotamus
Finished size: 5" x 7"

Make the inside of the card as interesting as the outside by using unique shapes.

Inside

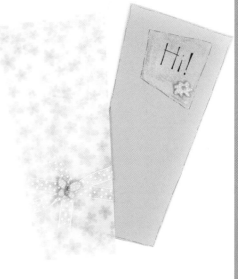

HI!

Jennifer Ellefson of Cranberry Township, Pennsylvania

Cardstock: Bazzill Basics
Vellum: Chatterbox
Ribbon: May Arts
Buttons: JHB International
Rub ons: Making Memories
Ink: Tsukineko
Pen: Zig
Embossing powder: Stampendous
Finished size: 8" (height), 4" (top) and 2 1/4" (bottom)

MOMENTS

Cindy Smith
of Knoxville, Maryland

Cardstock: **Bazzill Basics**
Pattern paper: **Carolee's Creations**
Leather frame: **EK Success**
Stickers: **Marcella by Kay**
Stamps: **Unknown**
Ribbon: **Craft supply**
Ink: **Ranger**
Finished size: **6" x 6"**

FRIENDS TAG

Cindy Smith of Knoxville, Maryland

Cardstock: **Bazzill Basics**
Staples: **Office supply**
Twill: **Unknown**
Stamps: **Impression Obsession and Outline Rubber Stamps**
Ink: **Rubber Stampede**
Finished size:
Tag: **2 1/2" x 4"**
Insert: **1 1/4" x 2 1/2"**

RED FLOWERS

Sharon Laakkonen of Superior, Wisconsin

Cardstock: Bazzill Basics
Pattern paper: Chatterbox
Frame: K & Company
Ribbon: Offray
Stamps and wax: Unknown
Finished size: 5 1/2" x 4 1/4"

Inside

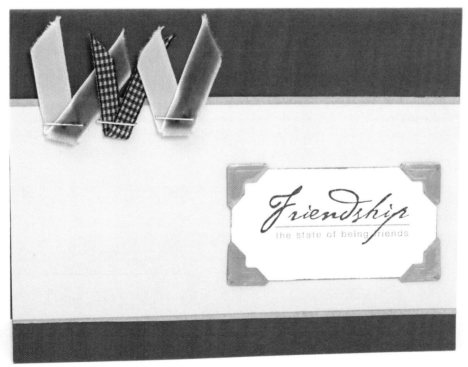

FRIENDSHIP

Janelle Richmond
of Dickinson, Texas

Cardstock: The Paper Company
Staples: Avery
Photo corners: Canson
Ribbon: Craft supply
Stickers: Making Memories
Ink: Ranger
Pens: Color Cutters
Finished size: 4 1/4" x 5 1/2"

Friendship
the state of being friends

53

for my friend

HELLO FRIEND
Tania Willis of Canton, Ohio

Cardstock: Die Cuts With a View
and Bazzill Basics
Pattern paper: KI Memories
and Die Cuts With a View
Staples: Office supply
Ribbon: May Arts and Offray
Punch: EK Success
Rub ons: Doodlebug Design
Ink: Ranger
Finished size: 5 1/2" x 5 1/2"

MISS YOU
Tania Willis of Canton, Ohio

Cardstock: Bazzill Basics
Punch: EK Success
Ink: Ranger
Floss: DMC
Pens: American Crafts
Finished size: 5 1/2" x 4 1/4"

SEASCAPE
Susan Weinroth of Philadelphia, Pennsylvania

Cardstock: Bazzill Basics
Brads and tag: Making Memories
Ribbon: Unknown
Stickers: Pebbles, Inc.
Ink: Ranger
Finished size: 5 3/4" x 5"

HELLO
Sharon Laakkonen
of Superior, Wisconsin

Cardstock: Bazzill Basics
Pattern paper and envelope: self-addressed.com
Ribbon: May Arts
Rub ons: Making Memories
Flowers: Prisma and Making Memories
Finished size: 6" x 6"

inside

MISS YOU

Susan Weinroth
of Philadelphia, Pennsylvania

Cardstock: Bazzill Basics
Pattern paper: 7 Gypsies
Brads: Making Memories
Stickers: Chatterbox
Ink: Ranger
Flower: Craft supply
Finished size: 6 1/4" x 5"

SECRETS

Terry Koehler of Olathe, Kansas

Cardstock: Bazzill Basics
Pattern paper: K & Company
Brad and lace: Craft supply
Pebble: K & Company
Petal: Making Memories
Stamps: Printworks
Finished size: 5 1/2" x 4 1/4"

IT MEANS SO MUCH
TO KEEP IN TOUCH
WITH SPECIAL
FRIENDS LIKE YOU

inside

HI
Sophia Corbridge

Cardstock: **Bazzill Basics**
Pattern paper: **Carolee's Creations**
Button: **SEI**
Stamps: **Image Tree**
Ink: **Close To My Heart**
Fiber: **DMC**
Finished size: 5 1/2" x 4 1/4"

FRIENDSHIP
Valerie Salmon of Carmel, Indiana

Card template: **Halcraft**
Cardstock: **Bazzill Basics**
Pattern paper: **American Crafts and KI Memories**
Flower: **Making Memories**
Buttons: **Unknown**
Finished size: 6 1/2" x 5"

Using a photograph on your card ensures that the card will be appreciated as much as a gift!

friends are like purses...
You can never have to many of them
thanks for being such a great person
Love ya,
Tina

FRIENDS ARE LIKE PURSES
Tina Gonzales

Cardstock: Bazzill Basics
Pattern paper: American Crafts
Die cut: My Mind's Eye
Button: Junkitz
Font: Quirky, downloaded from
twopeasinabucket.com
Finished size: 5" x 5"

FOR YOU
Sophia Corbridge

Cardstock: Bazzill Basics
Pattern paper and jute: SEI
Buttons: Making Memories and unknown
Charm: The Card Connection
Stamps: Hero Arts
Ink: Close To My Heart
Finished size: 5 1/2" x 4 1/4"

FORGET ME NOT
Terry Koehler of Olathe, Kansas

Cardstock: Bazzill Basics
Pattern paper: Karen Foster
Clip and chalk: Unknown
Pebble: K & Company
Stamps: Printworks
Finished size: 5 1/2" x 4 1/4"

inside

THANK YOU
Stefanie Gillins

Pattern paper: Kopp Design
Metal embellishment: Unknown
Ribbon: Offray
Finished size: 6 1/4" X 4 1/4"

THINKING OF YOU

Kristin Baxter of Valdosta, Georgia

Cardstock: Bazzill Basics
Pattern paper and die cuts: KI Memories
Brads, rub ons and metal tag: Making Memories
Ribbon: Offray and May Arts
Finished size: 4 1/4" x 5 1/2"

GET WELL SOON

Carolyn Lontin
of Highlands Ranch, Colorado

Cardstock: Archiver's
Pattern paper: KI Memories
Ribbon: May Arts
Ink: Memories
Font: International Palms, downloaded
from the internet
Finished size: 5 1/2" x 4 1/4"

Cards and tags are a great way to use
up those small scraps of ribbon. Store
like colors together in small, see-through
containers to make it easy to find just
what you need.

GET WELL

Sophia Corbridge

Pattern paper, tags and ribbon: SEI
Heart eyelet: Magic Scraps
Stamps: Hero Arts
Ink: Making Memories
Finished size: 4 1/4" x 5 1/2"

GET WELL
Tina Gonzales

Cardstock: Pebbles, Inc.
Pattern paper and stickers:
Karen Foster
Finished size: 4 1/4" x 5"

GET WELL
Tina Gonzales

Cardstock: **Bazzill Basics**
Pattern paper: **Reminisce**
Rub ons: **Creative Imaginations**
Stickers: **Karen Foster**
Finished size: 6" x 6"

GET WELL SOON
Rachael Giallongo of Auburn, New Hampshire

Cardstock: Bazzill Basics
Pattern paper and stickers: KI Memories
Brads and ribbon: adornedpages.com
Staples: Making Memories
Ink: StazOn
Finished size: 4 1/4" x 5 1/2"

GET WELL SOON
Sophia Corbridge

Cardstock: Bazzill Basics
Ribbon: SEI
Tag: Office supply
Stamps: Ma Vinci's Reliquary
Paint: Delta
Finished size: 6" x 6"

FEEL BETTER
Sophia Corbridge

Pattern paper, tag and ribbon: SEI
Stamps: Hero Arts
Ink: Making Memories
Finished size: 6" xv 6"

BRING ON
THE SUNSHINE
Sophia Corbridge

Pattern paper: O'Scrap! and SEI
Quote sticker: SEI
Buckle and ink: Making Memories
Ribbon: Offray
Finished size: 6" x 6"

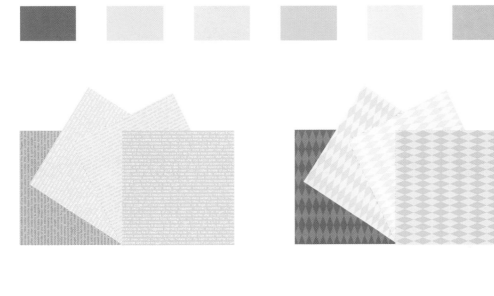
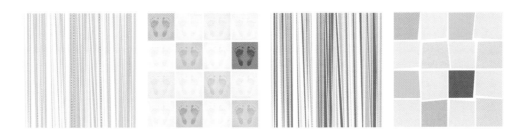

White Washed Nautical

extreme sport junkies

todd

trevor

july 2004

check it out

Wholesale information
866-254-1961

THE PAPER LOFT
www.paperloft.com
™

10 new cardstock patterns now available.

TRANSFORM PAPER INTO PURE IMAGINATION. ENTER FISKARS® GET READY, CRAFT!℠ CONTEST.

Receive honors and national recognition beyond your wildest dreams. Submit your favorite papercraft project and you could be selected to compete at The Craft & Hobby Association Show in Chicago, July 15–17, 2005. Mingle with papercraft's elite and take home the Grand Prize— a Fiskars® Craft Storage System, $1,000 of Fiskars® tools and significant public recognition.

Supported by:

Visit www.fiskars.com for additional locations.

Visit your local craft store or www.fiskars.com for an entry form. Entries will be accepted February 12–May 13, 2005.

GIVE THANKS

Kelli Dickinson of Des Moines, Iowa

Cardstock: Bazzill Basics
Pattern paper: KI Memories
Buckle: Junkitz
Ribbon: May Arts
Stickers: SEI
Stamps: MoBe' Stamps
Ink: Versacolor
Pen: Zig
Finished size: 4" x 5 3/4"

Instead of threading ribbon through a buckle, try tying a knot instead. This is a great way to use small scraps of ribbon and has a great look.

GIVE THANKS
Terry Koehler of Olathe, Kansas

Cardstock: **Chatterbox**
Pattern paper: **Sweetwater and Chatterbox**
Floss: **DMC**
Stamps: **Printworks**
Finished size: 5 1/2" x 4 1/4"

Rather than simply using adhesive to apply paper to a mat, stitch it on at the corners. Stitch the layers together before mounting to the card base with adhesive for added visual appeal.

GRATITUDE
Ramona Greenspan
of Yorktown Heights, New York

Cardstock: **Bazzill Basics**
Ribbon: **May Arts**
Rub ons: **Making Memories**
Stickers: **Pebbles, Inc.**
Finished size: 4 1/4" x 5 1/2"

BOO
Sophia Corbridge

Cardstock: Bazzill Basics
Paint: Making Memories
Stamps: PSX, Inkadinkado,
Ma Vinci's Reliquary and
Close To My Heart
Ink: Ranger
Ribbon: SEI
Finished size: 4 1/4" X 5 1/2"

HARVEST
Ramona Greenspan
of Yorktown Heights, New York

Cardstock and buttons: Bazzill Basics
Vellum: Chatterbox
Rub ons: Making Memories
Stickers: Pebbles, Inc.
Finished size: 5 1/2" x 4 1/4"

TRICK OR TREAT
Karen Bukovan of Odessa, Florida

Cardstock: Bazzill Basics
Ribbon: May Arts
Tags: Deluxe Designs
Finished size: 4" x 6"

HALLOWEEN MATCHBOOKS
by Alecia Grimm of Atlanta, Georgia

Cardstock: Bazzill Basics
Pattern paper: DMD Industries and 7 Gypsies
Transparency: K & Company
Staples: Office supply
Slide mounts: Loersch
Rub ons: Making Memories
Ink: Clearsnap and Rubber Stampede
Label maker: Dymo
Finished size: 2 1/2" x 3"

SNOW
Alisha Gordon

Cardstock and eyelets:
Bazzill Basics
Die cuts: My Mind's Eye
Snowflake brad and ribbon:
Making Memories
Finished size: 6" x 5 1/2"

WINTER
Alisha Gordon

Cardstock: Bazzill Basics
Die cuts: My Mind's Eye
Snowflake brad, ribbon charm
and ribbon: Making Memories
Finished size: 5" x 4 1/2"

CHANUKAH

Jennifer Harrison of Orem, Utah

Cardstock: **Pebbles, Inc.**
Pattern paper: **Making Memories**
Stamps: **Hero Arts and Stampin' Up!**
Ink: **Stampin' Up!**
Clear embossing medium: **Judikins**
Finished size: 4 1/2" x 4 1/4"

NEW YEAR'S

Cindy Smith of Knoxville, Maryland

Cardstock: Stampin' Up!
Ribbon: Unknown
Stickers: Die Cuts with a View
Ink: Versa Magic
Finished size: 5 1/2" x 4 1/4"

WINTER SNOW TAG

Sophia Corbridge

Pattern paper: O'Scrap!
Eyelet, tag and rub ons:
Making Memories
Stickers: SEI
Fibers: EK Success
Ink: Close To My Heart
Ribbon: Offray
Finished size: 5" x 2 1/2"

MOM

Candice Cruz
of Somerville, Massachusetts

Pattern paper, brads, washers, ribbon
and flower: **Making Memories**
Vellum envelope: **Unknown**
Tag: **Junkitz**
Ink: **StazOn**
Finished size: 6" x 4"

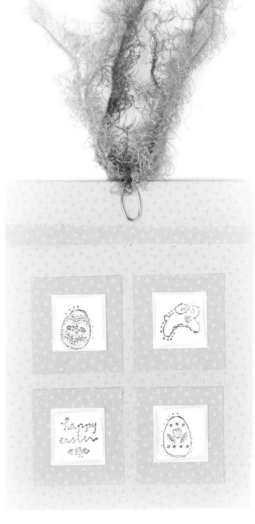

HAPPY EASTER

Sophia Corbridge

Pattern paper: **O'Scrap!**
Clip: **Making Memories**
Stamps: **Close To My Heart**
Chalk: **Creatacolor**
Fiber: **Unknown**
Finished size: 5 1/2" X 4 1/4"

Rather than punching a hole through
a card or tag, stitch or staple ribbons
and fibers for a new look. Paperclips
are also a great addition.

PRINCESS PARTY SET

by Cindy Smith of Knoxville, Maryland

Cardstock: Bazzill Basics and Stampin' Up!
Pattern paper: KI Memories
Ribbon: Michael's
Twill: Creative Impressions
Cake and princess stamps: Stampin' Up!
Phrase stamp: Magenta Stamps
Ink: Stamp Affair
Watercolor pencils: Crayola
Font: RagTag, downloaded
from twopeasinabucket.com
Finished size of card: 5 1/2" x 4 1/4"
Finished size of box: 3 1/4" x 6 1/2 x 2 1/2"

Please join us on Saturday June 11th

to celebrate Emma's First Birthday!

Where: Our Home

Time: One O'Clock

Phone: 301-123-4567

MIRACLE
Alisha Gordon

Cardstock: **Bazzill Basics**
Pattern paper: **Bo-Bunny Press**
Flower brad: **Provo Craft**
Foot brad: **Unknown**
White flowers: **Jolee's Boutique**
Flower and rub ons: **Making Memories**
Finished size: 5 3/4" x 5"

When attaching embellishments with brads, eyelets or nailheads, attach them to the top layers of matting before attaching the mat to the actual card base. The card will look as finished on the inside as on the outside.

IT'S A SHOWER
Jennifer Ellefson
of Cranberry Township, Pennsylvania

Card template: **Wordsworth**
Cardstock: **Bazzill Basics**
Tag and rub ons: **Making Memories**
Ribbon: **May Arts**
Buttons: **JHB International**
Pen: **Zig**
Fabric: **Fabric supply**
Finished size: 5 1/2" x 4 1/4"

CHIT-CHAT
Sophia Corbridge

Cardstock: Bazzill Basics
Pattern paper and die cut lettering:
Carolee's Creations
Stamp: Inkadinkado
Ink: Close To My Heart
Ribbon: SEI
Finished size: 5 1/2" x 4 1/4"

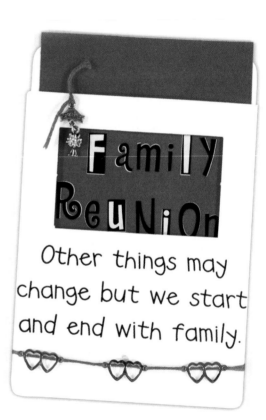

FAMILY REUNION
Tina Gonzales

Pocket: Kopp Design
Rub ons: Creative Imaginations
Charm: Art Accentz
Stamp: Rubber Stampede
Ink: Close To My Heart
Quote sticker: O'Scrap!
Floss: DMC
Finished size: 5 1/4" x 3 1/2"

PARTY

Summer Ford
of San Antonio, Texas

Pattern paper and fibers: **Basic Grey**
Charms: **Create a Craft**
Punch: **Fiskars**
Stamps and paint: **Making Memories**
Font: **Squish, downloaded from twopeasinabucket.com**
Finished size: **5 1/2" x 5 1/2"**

p.s. Leave your prince at home!

YOU'RE INVITED

Tina Gonzales

Cardstock: **Pebbles, Inc.**
Pattern paper and ribbon: **Doodlebug Design**
Label: **Making Memories**
Flower: **Reminisce**
Finished size: **5" x 5"**

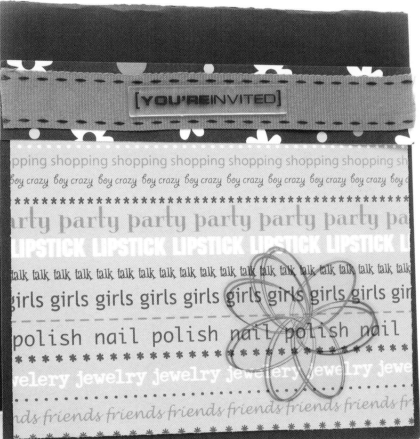

[YOU'RE INVITED]

PLEASE COME
Sophia Corbridge

Cardstock: **Bazzill Basics**
Pattern paper and Ribbon: **SEI**
Lettering stamps: **PSX**
Ink: **Ranger**
Finished size: 6" x 6"

For an extra special touch, place a band around the card to slide off before opening.

PLEASE COME
Sophia Corbridge

Cardstock: **Bazzill Basics**
Pattern paper: **SEI**
Eyelets: **Magic Scraps**
Rub ons: **Making Memories**
Ribbon: **EK Success**
Finished size: 4 1/4" x 5 1/2"

WHO, WHERE, WHEN

Sophia Corbridge

Pattern paper: **SEI**
Metal flowers: **Carolee's Creations**
Fiber: **Unknown**
Finished size: 5 1/2" x 4 1/4"

Place the message of the card in a pocket on the front and write any personal messages on the inside.

WATER PARTY

Tina Gonzales

Cardstock: **Bazzill Basics**
Cut outs: **My Mind's Eye**
Rub ons: **Scrapworks**
Finished size: 5 1/4" x 6 1/4"

COOL
Sophia Corbridge

Cardstock: Bazzill Basics
Pattern paper, buttons and ribbon: SEI
Ink: Close To My Heart
Finished size: 6" x 6"

HAPPY CAMPER

Miriam Campbell
of Olympia, Washington

Cardstock: The Paper Company
Pattern paper: KI Memories, SEI
and Leisure Arts
Concho: Scrapworks
Ribbon and jute: May Arts
Buttons: Chatterbox
Rub ons: Scrapworks
and Autumn Leaves
Stickers: K & Company, Bo-Bunny
Press and Doodlebug Design
Ink: Ranger
Label maker: Dymo
Finished size: 3" x 5 1/2"

HAPPY BIRTHDAY

Miki Benedict
of Modesto, California

Cardstock: Bazzill Basics
Pattern paper, eyelets and stickers:
Doodlebug Design
Fibers: Unknown
Tags: Making Memories
Stamps: Hero Arts
Ink: Memories and Ancient Page
Finished size: 5 1/2" x 5 1/2"

BE SWEET
Sophia Corbridge

Cardstock: Bazzill Basics
Stamps: Image Tree
Cut out: Disney
Ink and ribbon:
Close To My Heart
Finished size: 6" x 6"

HALLOWEEN GIFT TAGS
Sara Horton of Brownwood, Texas

Cardstock and tags: DMD Industries
Ribbon: Offray
Stamps: Peddler's Pack Stampworks
Ink: Clearsnap
Font: Picnic Basket, downloaded from twopeasinabucket.com
Spider ring: Craft supply
Finished size: 4 1/4" x 2"

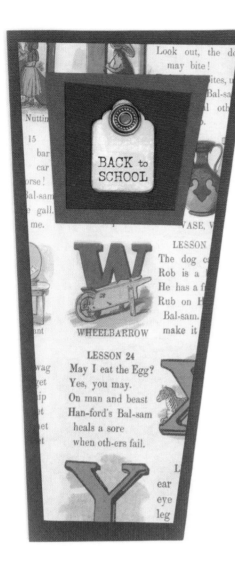

BACK TO SCHOOL
Stacy Stamitoles of Sylvania, Ohio

Cardstock: Bazzill Basics
Pattern paper: Design Originals
Brads and tag: Making Memories
Ink: All Night Media
Template: Wordsworth
Finished size: 8" tall, 4" across top and 2" at base.

SCOOBY DOO BIRTHDAY
Tami Mayberry of Lonedell, Missouri

Cardstock: Bazzill Basics and Worldwin
Pattern paper: Provo Craft
Brads: Making Memories
Rub ons: PSX
Stickers: Sandylion and-Bo Bunny Press
Finished size: 7" x 5"

85

THE LAUGHTER OF GIRLS

Tina Gonzales

Cardstock: Bazzill Basics
Pattern paper: Chatterbox
Cut outs: My Mind's Eye
Finished size: 4" x 6"

the **laughter** of **girls** is, and ever was, among the **delightful** sounds of the **earth**.

- de quincey

LITTLE PRINCESS CARD WITH CD

Tina Gonzales

Cardstock: Bazzill Basics
Pattern paper and CD: Chatterbox
Title cut out: My Mind's Eye
Finished size: 5 1/4" x 6 3/4"

PUPPY DOG TAILS
Tina Gonzales

Pattern paper and die cut: My Mind's Eye
Stickers: Pebbles, Inc.
Finished size: 4 1/2" x 4"

FAR OUT
Sophia Corbridge

Pattern paper, lettering and ribbon: SEI
Eyelet, clip and ink: Making Memories
Finished size: 5 1/4" x 4 1/4"

LOVE DEFINED

Stacey Kingman of Ellsworth, Illinois

Cardstock, brad and love charm: **Making Memories**
Pattern paper: **Rusty Pickle and Anna Griffin**
Ribbon: **May Arts**
Die cuts: **Autumn Leaves**
Stickers: **K & Company**
Ink: **Ranger**
Label maker: **Dymo**
Finished size: 4" x 5 1/2"

PROMISE ME

Rachael Giallongo
of Auburn, New Hampshire

Pattern paper and tag: Basic Grey
Transparency: Creative Imaginations
Staples: Making Memories
Ribbon: adornedpages.com
Rub on: Li'l Davis Designs
Ink: StazOn
Finished size: 4 1/4" x 5 1/2"

LUV YA

Helle Greer of Coronado, California

Cardstock: Bazzill Basics
Pattern paper: 7 Gypsies
Fibers: Unknown
Ribbon: May Arts and Offray
Mesh: Magic Mesh
Letter stamps: Hero Arts
Script stamp: Inkadinkado
Ink: Nick Bantock and ColorBox
Other: Vintage earring
Finished size: 5" x 7"

LOVE CARD & TAG
Melanie Cantrell of Olathe, Kansas

Cardstock: **Bazzill Basics**
Pattern paper: **Chatterbox and Melissa Frances**
Ribbon: **Offray**
Transparent stickers: **Cloud 9 Design**
Acrylic circles: **Sarah Heidt Photo Craft**
Stamps: **Impression Obsession**
Finished size of card: 5" x 5"
Finished size of tag: 2 3/4" x 5"

LOVE YOU
Tina Gonzales

Cardstock: **Bazzill Basics**
Tag: **Outdoors and More**
Mesh: **Avant Card**
Ribbon: **May Arts**
Finished size: 5 1/2" x 4 1/4"

XO

Tracy Michelitch
of Ashburn, Virginia

Pattern paper: Carolee's Creations,
7 Gypsies and KI Memories
Ribbon and jigsaw letters: Making Memories
Finished size: 5 1/2" x 4"

Brads, fancy buttons and charms
make great centers for blossoms.

LUV U

Shannon Bastian
of Haubstadt, Indiana

Cardstock: National
Pattern paper: 7 Gypsies
Brads: The Happy Hammer
and Making Memories
Acrylic label: Paperbilities
Die cut: Wish in the Wind
Flower: Craft supply
Stamps: Hero Arts
Ink: StazOn
Finished size: 5" x 5"

FOR MY LOVE

Melanie Cantrell
of Olathe, Kansas

Cardstock: Bazzill Basics
Pattern paper: 7 Gypsies
Metal letters: K & Company
Metal heart: EK Success
Paper clips: Office supply
Buttons: Craft supply
Ribbon: Offray
Woven letters:
me & my BIG ideas
Stickers: David Walker
for Creative Imaginations
Ink: Ranger
Finished size: 6" x 6 1/4"

LOVE YOU

Tina Gonzales

Cardstock: Bazzill Basics
Label: Making Memories
Fiber: May Arts
Ink: Hero Arts
Finished size: 2 3/4" x 4 1/2"

JAMES

Sara Bryans of Albany, New York

Cardstock: Bazzill Basics
Pattern paper: Chatterbox
Ribbon and makers: Stampin' Up!
Buttons: Junkitz
Tag and rub ons: Making Memories
Suede belt: Unknown
Finished size: 4" x 9 1/2"

SMITTEN

Tina Gonzales

Cardstock: Bazzill Basics
Frame and cut out:
My Mind's Eye
Label and charm:
Making Memories
Fiber: May Arts
Finished size: 5" x 6 1/2"

LOVE, LOVE
Sophia Corbridge

Cardstock: Bazzill Basics
Pattern paper: Karen Foster
Rub ons: Making Memories
Brads: Carolee's Creations
Ribbon: SEI
Finished size: 5 1/4" x 4 1/4"

Brads are a great way to attach the loose ends of a ribbon.

HAND IN HAND
Tania Willis of Canton, Ohio

Cardstock: Bazzill Basics
Pattern paper: Daisy D's
Staples: Office supply
Twist ties: Pebbles, Inc.
Ink: Ranger
Finished size: 5 1/2" x 4 1/4"

Putting a dab of glue along the ends of the ribbon will keep it from fraying.

LOVE
Sophia Corbridge

Cardstock: **Bazzill Basics**
Corners: **EK Success**
Cut out: **Carolee's Creations**
Finished size: 6" x 6"

Inexpensive notions from your local fabric supply can really "dress-up" your cards.

THOUGHTFUL
Terry Koehler of Olathe, Kansas

Cardstock: **Bazzill Basics**
Pattern paper: **The Vintage Workshop**
Vellum: **Unknown**
Buttons: **K & Company**
Ribbon: **Model Crafts**
Stamps: **Printworks**
Finished size: 5 1/2" x 4 1/4"

inside

Love Inside

Shortcuts to Fabulous Cards

Sophia Corbridge

DARE TO DREAM

Cardstock: Bazzill Basics
File folder: Rusty Pickle
Rub ons:
Making Memories
Eyelet: Magic Scraps
Stamp: Inkadinkado
Ink: Ranger
Ribbon: SEI
Finished size:
4 1/4" x 5 3/4"

SIMPLE JOYS

Cardstock:
Bazzill Basics
Pattern paper and
embellishment:
K & Company
Vellum quote:
Die Cuts
with a View
Nailhead:
Westrim Crafts
Ribbon: SEI
Finished size:
6" x 6"

Our lives are filled
with **simple** joys
and blessings without end.
But one of the **greatest**
joys in life
is to have you as a
friend.

Almost twenty years ago I received a darling gift, a tiny bird figurine on a mailbox with an envelope peeking out. The envelope was labeled "Love inside." Though that figurine is long gone, the thought still enters my mind whenever I open my mailbox and find a hand written address on an envelope. The sight of that envelope brings the anticipation of the "love inside."

I recently received a beautiful hand-made card from a longtime friend. It truly warmed my heart! Ironically, we ran into each other while out to dinner later that same evening. I thanked her for her darling card and her husband proudly announced, "You should see how many cards she's made!" His pride in his wife's efforts was very evident and I could hardly wait to get home and look at her card again. Although she works full-time, she still keeps a wonderful home and finds time to create beautiful layouts and cards for her friends. Like my friend, we could all use a few extra hours in our day just to have time to be creative. However, by learning to make simple, quick and easy cards, we can fit creating a card into our already busy schedule. By using a few shortcuts, your cards can include lots of "love inside" without taking so much of your precious time!

YOU'RE SO SWEET

Cardstock: Bazzill Basics
Pattern paper and rub on: SEI
Charm: Carolee's Creations
Finished size: 4 1/4" x 5 1/4"

THANKS

Cardstock, buttons, ribbon and cut out: SEI
Stamp: Stampin' Up!
Ink: Close To My Heart
Finished size: 6" x 6"

HOLLY JOLLY CHRISTMAS

Cardstock: Bazzill Basics
Cut out and charm: All My Memories
Mitten and sticker: Unknown
Ribbon: SEI
Finished size: 5 1/2" x 4 1/4"

HAPPY BIRTHDAY

Cardstock: Bazzill Basics
Pattern paper: Bo-Bunny Press
Shaker: Carolee's Creations
Ribbon and ink: Close To My Heart
Finished size: 4 1/4" x 5 1/4"

To create quick and easy cards and tags, THINK SHORTCUTS! With all of the great pre-made accents and embellishments available today, things are easier than ever. Add your own personal touch to pre-made embellishments by using ink, chalk, pens, buttons, ribbons, fiber and half the work is already done for you.

✎ Put your computer fonts to work. Share special thoughts, quotes and heartfelt messages in your cards. If you don't care for your own handwriting, a few fun fonts are a must.

✎ Include song lyrics or poetry just as store-bought cards do.

✎ Buy the full line of a product. Most of your decision making is done for you in advance. Sometimes selecting the colors and co-ordinating paper takes as much time as creating the card. Let the paper artists and designers make that step easy by buying their entire line. Your job will be as simple as picking and choosing which products you want to use.

✎ For a different approach, select a few accents from your stash and then decide what to do with them, rather than trying everything until you find something that works. Pick three or four items and simply arrange them on the card. The card, in essence, builds itself!

✎ When creating several of the same card, use small blocks of free time and work a step at a time, assembly-line style. If you have a few extra minutes during a phone call or while waiting for the pasta to boil, score and fold all of the cards. Next break, attach any metals. Breaking each card into smaller steps allows you to create many of the same card in no time at all.

✎ Use letter or word rub-ons. They are quick and easy, no mess and always look great! Don't worry about having things aligned perfectly. Your own handwriting would not be and besides that, it adds a personal touch to your card.

✎ Don't fret over perfection. Each card is your own masterpiece in the eyes of the recipient.

✎ Cards are a great place to use things like staples, brads and larger metal pieces since you don't have to worry about damaging photos.

✎ Rubber stamps are one of the fastest ways to create a great personal card, especially when mass producing cards. Purchase stamps that will

100

work for more than one card and use it as often as you can. One stamp I have used in dozens of different cards is an old clock face stamp that makes a great background on any card. Find a few favorite stamps and use them over and over!

"Goofs" from scrapping can always be put to use on a card. If the tag didn't fit or wasn't quite what you wanted on a layout, save it for a simple and quick card when you are in a hurry.

Simple cards can be the most elegant. With just the right paper and a simple ribbon and embellishment, a card can be created in moments.

Keep a file of cards created by others for inspiration the next time you sit down to make cards. One element might spark your creativity.

Whenever possible, create a duplicate card to have one on hand when you need it at a moment's notice.

Think outside the box. A birthday candle flame could be created out of anything from a button to a french knot to a heart shaped brad.

Fold your card differently for a little extra flair.

A pin, necklace or charm can be attached to a card as the gift itself.

Life doesn't always allow us the time to create "works of art" for each card we make. However, you can create "works of heart" using a few moments, a few supplies and a little creativity. You'll feel the love inside each handmade card you make!

FRIEND

Kelli Dickinson of Des Moines, Iowa

Cardstock: Bazzill Basics
Pattern paper: KI Memories
Ink: Versacolor
Finished size: 5" x 7"

HI
Sophia Corbridge

Cardstock: **Bazzill Basics**
Pattern paper, vellum, ribbon and
coasters: **SEI**
Eyelets: **Magic Scraps**
Finished size: 6" x 6"

Overlap the coasters, then
attach by setting eyelets. Tie
them together with a ribbon
before mounting to the card.

MAKE A WISH
Kristin Baxter of Valdosta, Georgia

Pattern paper: **KI Memories**
Ribbon: **Offray**
Stickers: **Making Memories**
Finished size: 5 1/2" x 4 1/2"

133

NOEL

Wendy Inman of Virginia Beach, Virginia

Cardstock: Bazzill Basics
Rub ons: Making Memories
Slide mount: Deluxe Designs
Finished size: 4" x 6"

ENJOY

Amy Smith
of Los Angeles, California

Cardstock: Die Cuts with a View
Brads: Creative Imaginations
Washer and tag:
Making Memories
Ribbon and flower: Craft supply
Finished size: 5" x 7"

ENJOY
Karen Bukovan of Odessa, Florida

Cardstock: **Bazzill Basics**
Stickers: **Making Memories and Pebbles, Inc.**
Finished size: 5 1/2" x 4 1/4"

Cards that are quick and easy to produce are perfect for holiday greetings, baby announcements, and any other occasion where you need multiple cards.

SUGAR & SPICE
Liz Taylor of Richfield, Utah

Cardstock: **Memory Lane**
Pattern paper: **SEI**
Twill: **Unknown**
Stamps: **Rusty Pickle and Hero Arts**
Ink: **Close To My Heart**
Finished size: 4" x 5 1/2"

FLOWER

Shannon Bastian
of Haubstadt, Indiana

Cardstock: National
Pattern paper, sticker and button: SEI
Flower: Craft supply
Finished size: 4 1/4 x 5 1/2"

HI

Christine Traversa,
of Joliet, Illinois

Card template: Gartner Studios
Cardstock: Georgia Pacific and unknown
Metal word charm: K & Company
Punch: Family Treasures
Stamp: Denami Design
Ink: Stampin' Up!

HI
Sophia Corbridge

Cardstock: Bazzill Basics
Pattern paper and charm:
All My Memories
Rub ons and ink:
Making Memories
Ribbon: SEI
Finished size: 4 1/4" x 5 1/2"

SIMPLIFY
Sophia Corbridge

Cardstock: Bazzill Basics
Pattern paper: Basic Grey
Tag: Making Memories
Stamp and ink: Close To My Heart
Ribbon: SEI
Finished size: 5 1/2" x 4 1/4"

THINKING OF YOU

Dana Smith of Eden Prairie, Minnesota

Cardstock, pattern paper, rub ons, nails and die cut tag: **Chatterbox**
Finished size: 5 1/2" x 4 1/4"

WITH SYMPATHY

Carolyn Lontin
of Highlands Ranch, Colorado

Cardstock: Bazzill Basics and craft supply
Pattern paper: Die Cuts with a View
Ribbon: May Arts
Ink: Memories
Font: International Palms, downloaded from
the internet
Finished size: 5 1/2" x 4 1/4"

THINKING OF YOU

Wendy Malichio of Bethel, Connecticut

Pattern paper, decorative hinge, ribbon and stickers:
Paper House Productions
Font: Carpenter, downloaded from the internet and Bernie
Finished size: 8 1/2" x 5 1/2"

THINKING OF YOU

Sophia Corbridge

Pattern paper and ribbon: SEI
Charm: Carolee's Creations
Brads: All My Memories
Stamp: Close To My Heart
Ink: Ranger
Finished size: 4 1/4" x 5 1/2"

THINKING OF YOU
Jennifer Miller of Humble, Texas

Cardstock: Bazzill Basics
Pattern paper: KI Memories
Sticker: Pebbles, Inc.
Font: Marydale, downloaded from the internet
Finished size: 4" x 5 1/2"

Thinking of You

THINKING OF YOU
Sophia Corbridge

Cardstock: Bazzill Basics
Pattern paper: K & Company
Glass embellishment: EK Success
Rub ons and ink: Making Memories
Finished size: 5 1/2" x 4 1/4"

thinking
of you

THINKING OF YOU
Sophia Corbridge

Cardstock: Bazzill Basics
Pattern paper and Brads: Carolee's Creations
Flower embellishment: K & Company
Stamp: Provo Craft
Ink: Close To My Heart
Ribbon: SEI
Finished size: 5 1/2" x 4 1/4"

Tear the edge of the front of the card. Rub an ink pad along the edges of the torn paper to accentuate the tear for a great look.

THINKING OF YOU
Sophia Corbridge

Cardstock: Bazzill Basics
Pattern paper:
Making Memories
Flower brad: Unknown
Lettering stamps: PSX
Ink: Ranger
Ribbon: SEI
Finished size: 4 1/4" x 5 1/2"

THANK YOU
Wendy Inman of Virginia Beach, Virginia

Cardstock: Bazzill Basics
Pattern paper: KI Memories
Brads: Unknown
Die cuts: Legacy Paper Arts
Rub ons: Making Memories
Finished size: 4 1/4" x 5 1/2"

THANK YOU

Andrea Cox
of Hillsville, Virginia

Pattern paper: Basic Grey
Mosaic tiles: Sara Heidt
Ribbon: Offray
Rub ons: Making Memories
Ink: ColorBox
Finished size: 4 1/4" x 5 1/2"

THANKS

Sara Bryans of Albany, New York

Cardstock: Bazzill Basics
Pattern paper: Chatterbox
Floss: DMC
Rub ons: Making Memories
Finished size: 4 1/4" x 5 1/2"

THANK YOU

Susan Weinroth
of Philadelphia, Pennsylvania

Cardstock and brads: Bazzill Basics
Pattern paper: NRN Designs
and KI Memories
Stickers: Creative Imaginations
Finished size: 5" x 5 1/4"

THANK YOU

Stacey Kingman of Ellsworth, Illinois

Cardstock: Bazzill Basics
Pattern paper: Paper Fever
Ribbon: May Arts, me & my BIG ideas
and craft supply
Die cuts and acrylic accents: KI Memories
Finished size: 4 1/4" x 5 1/2"

THANK YOU

Stacey Kingman
of Ellsworth, Illinois

Cardstock: **Close To My Heart**
Pattern paper: **KI Memories
and unknown**
Ribbon: **May Arts and Offray**
Die cuts: **KI Memories**
Stickers: **Doodlebug Design**
Ink: **Ranger**
Label maker: **Dymo**
Finished size: **4" x 5 1/2"**

THANK YOU

Amy Smith
of Los Angeles, California

Cardstock: **Neenah**
Punches: **Marvy Uchida**
Die cuts: **KI Memories**
Rub ons: **Doodlebug Design**
Stickers: **American Crafts**
Finished size: **4 3/4" x 4 3/4"**

THANK YOU

Tania Willis of Canton, Ohio

Cardstock: Bazzill Basics
Pattern paper: Chatterbox
Staples: Office supply
Stamps: PSX and Hero Arts
Fluid chalk: Clearsnap
Circle punch: EK Success
Finished size: 5 1/2 x 4 1/4"

Attach embellishments with staples, stitches or bows.

THANK YOU

Wendy Malichio of Bethel, Connecticut

Cardstock: Bazzill Basics
Pattern paper and transparencies: Paper House Productions
Ribbon: Bobbin Ribbon
Fonts: Aquiline and Times New Roman
Finished size: 5" x 6"

THANK YOU
Sheredian Vickers

Cardstock: Bazzill Basics
Pattern paper: Karen Foster
Ribbon: Offray
Stamps: Hero Arts
Ink: Stampabilities
Corner rounder punch:
Marvy Uchida
Finished size: 5 1/2" x 4"

THANKS
Tania Willis of Canton, Ohio

Cardstock: Bazzill Basics
Pattern paper: Chatterbox
Safety pin: Making Memories
Fibers and buttons: Hill Creek Designs
Ribbon: May Arts
Stamps: PSX
Ink: Ranger
Finished size: 5 1/4" x 4 1/4"

THANKS

Lucy Marino
of Downington, Pennsylvania

Cardstock, pattern paper, rub ons
and woven label: **Making Memories**
Clip: **Scrapworks**
Ink: **Close To My Heart**
Finished size: 4 1/4" x 5 1/2"

inside

For a unique look, make a slit in the mat and attach the
paper clip in the center of the card rather than the edge.

THX
Sophia Corbridge

Cardstock: Bazzill Basics
Pattern paper: K & Company
Rub on: Making Memories
Metal plaque: EK Success
Ribbon: SEI
Ink: Ranger
Tag: Office supply
Finished size: 4 1/4" x 5 1/2"

Rub-on letters can be easily applied to metal plaques, in addition to cardstock and pattern paper.

MANY THANKS
Sophia Corbridge

Cardstock: Bazzill Basics
Lettering cut outs: Carolee's Creations
Rub ons: Making Memories
Metal plaque: EK Success
Ribbon: SEI
Finished size: 4 1/4" x 8 1/2"

Place lettering blocks randomly along the edge of the card, then trim the card at the bottom of the blocks.

119

THANK YOU
Tina Gonzales

Pattern paper and frame: My Mind's Eye
Rub ons: Making Memories
Finished size: 5 3/4" x 7 1/2"

FOR ALL YOU DO...
Ralonda Heston of Murfreesboro, Tennesse

Pattern paper and tags: Basic Grey
Conchos and die cuts: Scrapworks
Ribbon: Making Memories
Stickers: Wordsworth
Pen: Staedtler
Finished size: 5 1/2" x 4 1/2"

Stitch along the fold for a "binding" on your card.

THANKS
Sophia Corbridge

Cardstock:
Bazzill Basics
Pattern paper:
Karen Foster
Eyelet, stamps
and metal letter:
Making Memories
Brad: Carolee's Creations
Lettering sticker:
Rusty Pickle
Rub ons: EK Success
Tag: Office supply
Ink: Close To My Heart
Finished size:
4 1/4" x 8 1/2"

THANK YOU
Sophia Corbridge

Cardstock: **Bazzill Basics**
Pattern paper, ribbon and jute: **SEI**
Corrugated paper: **DMD Industries**
Brad: **Carolee's Creations**
Tag and clips: **Making Memories**
Stamp: **Unknown**
Ink: **Close To My Heart**
Finished size: 6" x 6"

THANK YOU
Tina Gonzales

Cardstock: **It Takes Two**
Pattern paper: **Chatterbox**
Charm: **Making Memories**
Finished size: 3" x 4"

Scraps of different papers, ribbon and metal will add a unique texture to your cards.

a Bazzillion

colors, ideas & products to make your creations DAZZLE!

Paper

Albums

Envelopes

Brads

Buttons

Boshers

Idea Books

Bazzill Chips

Bazzill Basics Paper™

REAL SWEET

480.558.8557   fax 480 558-8558   www.BazzillBasics.com

MAKE IT GENUINE!

Art Warehouse Denim Word

Art Warehouse Transparency

Art Warehouse Paper

Art Warehouse License Plate

Art Warehouse I.D. Plate

Introducing the NEW Genuine Collection from Art Warehouse!

From Papers, Stickers, Metal License Plates, Metal I.D. Plates, Metal Photo Corners, Denim Tags & Denim Words to coordinating Bazzill Basics Genuine Cardstock Multi-pack, it's easy to make your scrapbook pages genuine!

Ask for Genuine Collection at your favorite scrapbook store!

www.cigift.com • 1-800-942-6487 wholesale orders only

NEW!

ALABAMA

**THE RUBBER STAMP
LADY, INC**
7914 MEMORIAL PARKWAY SW
HUNTSVILLE, AL 35802
256-880-1106
Fax 256-880-1129
www.rubberstamplady.com

ARKANSAS

1 MOMENT IN TIME
3400 ROGERS AVE. #120
FORT SMITH, AR 72903
479-494-5655
www.onescrapbookstore.com
m,t,th-sat 10-9 wed
10-6 sun 1-5

ARIZONA

**PAPER & METAL
SCRAPPERS**
804 N BEELINE HWY
PAYSON, AZ 85341
928-468-1188
paperandmetal@earthlink.net

SCRAPBOOK BARN
949 N. VAL VISTA DR. STE A-115
GILBERT, AZ 85234
480-503-2475
www.scrapbookbarn.com

SCRAPBOOKS, ETC
2820 E. UNIVERSITY DR. #111
MESA, AZ 85213
480-854-2303
scrapbooksetc@qwest.net
www.scrapbooks-etc.com

CALIFORNIA

ONCE UPON A PAGE
2800 W. BURBANK BLVD
BURBANK, CA 91505
818-846-8910
onceuponapage@aol.com
www.onceuponapage.com

ONCE UPON A TIME
780 N MAIN ST.
CORONA, CA 92880
909-372-8214
m-f 10:30-6 sat 11-5 sun 12-4

SCRAP THAT IDEA!
2440 SANDCREEK ROAD STE E5
BRENTWOOD, CA 94513
925-516-8522
m-sat 10-7 sun 12-4
scrapthatidea@aol.com

SCRAPBOOK BLESSINGS
2233 MICHAEL DR
NEWBURY PARK, CA 91320
805-375-1568
service@scrapbookblessings.com
www.scrapbookblessings.com

SCRAPBOOK NOOK
444 SAN MATEO AVE.
SAN BRUNO, CA 94066
650-588-3112
www.myscrapbooknook.com

SCRAPPERS ANONYMOUS
832 W. TEXAS ST.
FAIRFIELD, CA 94533
707-435-1700
scrapperdetox@aol.com

**SCRAPPIN' WITH
MOMMY & ME**
2401-A SAN PABLO AVE.
PINOLE, CA 94564
510-724-2010
m-sat 10-7 sun 10-5

STAMPERS WAREHOUSE
101 G TOWN & COUNTRY DR
DANVLLE, CA 94526
925-362-9595
customerservice@
stamperswarehouse.com
www.stamperswarehouse.com

THE KEEPSAKE COMPANY
310 3RD AVE STE A5
CHULA VISTA, CA 91910
619-427-6594
m-f 10-6 sat 11-4

THE PAPER RABBIT
2269 HONOLULU AVE
MONTROSE, CA 91020
818-957-2848
scribbles1@earthlink.net
www.thepaperrabbit.com

COLORADO

**KEEPSAKES AND
MEMORIES**
1240 KEN PRATT BLVD. #7
LONGMONT, CO 80501
808-774-7895
ek elite store
www.keepsakesandmemories.net

THE TREASURE BOX
1833 E HARMONY RD#1
FORT COLLINS, CO 80528
970-207-9939
treasbox@msn.com

CONNECTICUT

**NEW ENGLAND
SCRAPBOOK CO.**
200 ALBANY TURNPIKE RTE 44
CANTON, CT 06019
860-693-9197
m-tu 10-6 w-th 10-9 f-sat 10-10
sun 12-5
www.newenglandscrapbook.com

GEORGIA

SCRAPBOOK OUTLET
PRIME OUTLETS AT CALHOUN
#56
455 BELWOOD RD
CALHOUN, GA 49424
706-602-3555
I-75 between Atlanta &
Chattanooga

125

IDAHO

IT'S ALL ABOUT ME
2615 KOOTENAI
BOISE, ID 83705
208-387-2767
m-sat 10-7
www.scrapbookwithmarianne.com
fax- 208-387-4990

OBG'S UNDERGROUND
SCRAPBOOKING SUPPLY CO.
COEUR D'ALENE, ID
280-664-6010
www.obgunderground.com
open house: tues 9-3 all days,
other days call for an appointment

SCRAPPIN' ON THE
BOULEVARD
1520 NORTHWEST BOULEVARD
COEURD'ALENE, ID 83814
208-765-3994
m-f 10-6 sat 10-5 sun 11-4
www.scrappinontheboulevard.com
scrappinontheboulevard@msn.com

TIFFANY SQUARE
132 MAIN AVE. NORTH
TWIN FALLS, ID 83301
208-736-7286
fax 208-736-8592

ILLINOIS

IMAGINE SCRAPBOOKING
& STAMPING
901 SOUTH NEIL ST. STE B
CHAMPAIGN, IL 61820
217-352-0532
imaginescrapbook@aol.com
www.scrapbookingillinois.com

SCRAPBOOK LANE
3033 THEODORE STREET
JOLIET, IL 60435
815-577-6789
www.scrapbooklane.net
m-fri 10-8 sat 10-6 sun 11-5

WINDY CITY
SCRAPBOOKING
2265 N CLYBOURN AVE
CHICAGO, IL 60614
773-935-0585
info@windycityscrapbooking.com
www.windycityscrapbooking.com

INDIANA

CREATIVE CORNER
SCRAPBOOKS
520 N STATE ROAD 135
GREENWOOD, IN 46142
317-883-2177
friends@creativecornerscrapbooks.com
www.creativecornerscrapbooks.com

SCHMITT PHOTO
4847 PLAZA EAST BLVD
EVANSVILLE, IN 47715
m-fri 8:30-8 sat 9-6 sun 1-5
www.schmittphoto.com

SCRAPBOOK MAGIC
122 CREEKSIDE DR. (ON U.S. 31)
KOKOMO, IN 46901
765-868-9263
sbmagic@sbsglobal.net

SCRAPBOOK OUTLET
PRIME OUTLETS SOUTH #10
FREMONT, IN 46737
260-833-2767
I-69 and 80/90 Toll Road

SCRAPBOOK XANADU
9719 E US. HWY 36
AVON, IN 46123
(317) 209-6000
m-f 10-9 sat 10-7 sun 12-5
www.scrapbookxanadu.com

SCRAPBOOK XANADU 2
5459 E. 82ND ST.
INDIANAPOLIS, IN 46250
(317) 579-2500
m-f 10-9 sat 10-7 sun 12-5
www.scrapbookxanadu.com

IOWA

HEIRLOOMS BY DESIGN
213 FIFTH ST
WEST DES MOINES, IA 50265
515-274-3602
stamp@qwest.net
www.heirloomsbydesign.com

MEMORY BOUND
SCRAPBOOK STORE
E.K. ELITE STORE
641 N ANKENY BLVD
ANKENY, IA 50021
515-965-1102
www.memorybound.com

MEMORY BOUND
SCRAPBOOK STORE
819 WHEELER STE 6
AMES, IA 50010
505-233-6411
m,w 9:30-6 tu,th 9:30-8 sat 9:30-5
sun 12-4
www.memorybound.com

MAINE

FROZEN IN TIME
175 MAIN STREET STE 103
MADAWASKA, ME 04756
207-728-6449

MARYLAND

JUST CROP IT!
5624 RANDOLPH RD.
ROCKVILLE, MD 20852
301-770-2368
m,th 10:30-6 w,fri,
sat 10:30-8 sun 11-5
www.justcropit.net

MASSACHUSETTS

MEMORY LANE
449 WASHINGTON ST
WEYMOUTH, MA 02188
781-335-0007
t, thu 10-9 w, fri, sat 10-5
lynettecarroll@comcast.net

MICHIGAN

MAGGIE'S SCRAPBOOK HEAVEN
104 W. WACKERLY, STE B
MIDLAND, MI 48640
989- 835-5577

SCRAPBOOK 101
5169 HARVEY STREET
MUSKEGON, MI 49441
231-798-7373
www.scrapbook101.com

MINNESOTA

CRAFTS DIRECT
620 SUNDIAL DR
WAITE PARK, MN 56387
800-784-8868
m-f 9-9 sat 9-8 sun 10-6

MEMORY BOX
38 N. UNION ST
MORA, MN 55051
320-679-3439
memorybox@ncis.com

PRETTY IN INK
1425 129TH AVE NE
BLAIN, MN 55434
763-755-9544
m-f 10-8 sat10-6 sun 12-4
www.prettyinink.com

SCRAPBOOKS LTD
1095 DIFFLEY RD
EAGAN, MN 55123
651-905-3995

NEBRASKA

MEMORY LANE SCRAPBOOK
AND BED & BREAKFAST
49144 W. BENTON ST.
O'NEILL, NE 68763
(1/4 mile N. of the Westside
Restaurant)
402-488-8860
m 12-6 tu,th 12-8 w,f 10-6 sat 10-5

NEVADA

PEBBLES IN MY POCKET
4880 E. BONANZA #4
LAS VEGAS, NV 89110
702-438-9080
sun 10-2 m-wed 10-3
th-f 10-3,6-11 sat 10-5

NEW YORK

SCRAPBOOK CITY
1022 UNION ROAD
WEST SENICA, NY 14224
716-677-5650
www.scrapbookcity.com

NORTH CAROLINA

A PAGE IN TIME
1004 CORPORATE DR.
GOLDSBORO, NC 27530
919-580-9300
Arlene@apgntime.com
www.apgntime.com

OHIO

CROP-PAPER-SCISSORS
3583 MEDINA RD
MEDINA, OH. 44256
330-723-6171
m 10-5 tu-f 10-8 sat 10-6 sun 1-5
www.crop-paper-scissors.com
cpsinc@zoominternet.net

SCRAPBOOK HEAVEN
210 CLINTON ST.
DEFIANCE, OH 43512
419-782-7001
croproom@scrapbookheaven.net
www.scrapbookheaven.net

SCRAPBOOK OUTLET
PRIME OUTLETS AT LODI #215
9909 AVON LAKE RD
BURBANK, OH
330-948-8080
I-71 20 miles South of Cleveland

SCRAPPERS' DELIGHT SCRAPBOOK SUPERSTORE
5923 HOOVER RD
GROVE CITY, OH 43123
614-277-2767
info@scrappersdelight.com
www.scrappersdelight.com

OKLAHOMA

SIMPLY SCRAPBOOKS
991 W. WILL RODGERS BLVD
CLAREMORE, OK 74017
918-343-5553
m-sat 10-6 th 10-8 sun 1-5
www.simplyscrapbooksok.com

OREGON

MEMORIES OF TIME
300 CENTRAL AVE
COOS BAY, OR 97420
541-269-1053

SCATTERED PICTURES
13852 NE SANDY BLVD
PORTLAND, OR 97230
503-252-1888
tu-th-f 10-5 w-10-8 sat 10-4
closed sun & mon

SCRAP-A-DOODLE
2220 NE HWY 20 #1
BEND, OR 97701
541-388-0311
scrapyard@empnet.com
www.scrap-a-doodle.com

PENNSYLVANIA

SCRAPBOOK SUPERSTATION
168 POINT PLAZA ROUTE 356 & 68
BUTLER, PA 16001
724- 287-4311
m-sat 10-9 sun 12-5
www.scrapbookstation.com

SOUTH CAROLINA

SCRAPBOOK CONCEPT
804 J. SECOND LOOP RD
FLORENCE, SC 29505
843-665-9624
m-fri 10-6 sat 10-4
scrapbookconcept@sc.rr.com

SCRAPBOOKS EXPRESS INC
2443 E. CHERRY RD
ROCK HILL, SC 29732
803-329-3227
www.scrapbooks-express.com

TEXAS

NOVEL APPROACH
607 S. FRIENDSWOOD DR. #15
FRIENDSWOOD, TX 77546
281-992-3137
www.booksandscraps.com

THE SCRAPBOOK VILLAGE
3424 FM 1092, STE 270
MISSOURI CITY, TX 77459
281-208-5251
scrapbookvillage@yahoo.com
www.thescrapbookvillage.com

VIRGINIA

SCRAPBOOK PLUS
13908 METROTECH DR.
CHANTILLY, VA 20151
703-266-2450
m-sat 10-9 sun 12-5
www.scrapbooks-plus.com

SCRAPDOODLES
1315 CENTRAL PARK BLVD
FREDERICKSBURG, VA 22401
540-548-3788
m-sat 10-9 sun 12-5
www.scrapdoodles.com

WASHINGTON

A LITTLE BIT OF HEAVEN
7912 MARTINWAY EAST
OLYMPIA, WA 98516
360-493-1707

PAGE BY PAIGE
32 N. MAIN ST.
OMAK, WA 98841
509-422-2383
pagebypaige@ncidata.com
www.pagebypaige.net

WISCONSIN

BEN FRANKLIN
317 MALL DR.
APPLETON, WI 54915
920-735-1702

MEMORY JUNCTION
2217 SILVERMAIL RD
PEWAUKEE, WI 53072
262-542-8467
info@memoryjunction.com
www.memoryjunction.com

THAT SCRAPBOOKING PLACE
435 E MILL ST. UNIT 18
PLYMOUTH, WI 53073
920-892-2919
www.thatscrapbookingplace.com

CANADA

DALCRAFTS
1855 PEMBINA HWY
WINNIPEG, CANADA R3T2G6
204-275-2204
m,w,f,sat 10-6 t, th 10-9 sun 12-4
www.dalcrafts.com

PHOTO EXPRESS
100 – 22470 DEWDNEY TRUNK RD
MAPLE RIDGE, B.C. CANADA
V2X5Z6
604-463-3654
photoexpress@telus.net
www.photoexpressfotosource.ca

advertising directory

BAZZILL BASICS	122
CREATIVE IMAGINATIONS	123
FISKARS	67
NRN DESIGNS	130
PAPER LOFT	66
PAPER TRENDS	124
PIONEER PHOTO	3
ST ONLINE	131
ST PAPER	65
ST SUBSCRIBE	129
SCRAPJAMMIES	2
SCRAPWORKS	6

YOURS IS A HISTORY IN THE MAKING.

[And much more exciting than those old 101 books still sitting in your closet!]

Get inspiration and motivation for preserving your history from Scrapbook Trends every month! Subscribe today!

Subscribe by Mail: P.o. Box 1570 Orem, UT 84059   Subscribe by Phone: 888.225.9199   Subscribe Online: www.scrapbooktrendsmag.com

- -

☐ 1 year $24.97   ☐ 2 year $44.97   ☐ 3 year $62.97

Name

Address

City   State/Prov.   Zip/Postal Code

Country   E-Mail Address

Credit Card Number   Expiration Date   Signature

☐ Bill Me Later (Add $2 for processing)   ☐ Payment Enclosed   ☐ Charge My: Visa_____ MC_____ Amex. _____ Discover _____

Canadian and Mexico orders, Please add $10/year postage. All other countries, please add $18/year. US Funds only, please. Please allow 6-8 weeks for delivery of your first issue.